Echoes Through the Spiral:

A Soul's Continuum

Gia

ROOTED HOUND
PRESS

First published by Rooted Hound Publishing
© 2025 by Gia

ISBN: 978-1-969687-02-0
Printed in the United States of America

To my husband — for your unwavering love, understanding, and endless patience with me during this journey of awakening and writing. I could not have done this without you.

Preface

"I didn't set out to write a book. I was trying to understand my own becoming."

This book wasn't written from a mountaintop or a meditation cushion. It was written in the middle of life — in stress, in echoes, in the very spirals I describe.

I used to worry about what people might think, especially those who appear in these pages in one way or another. But I've realized something important: I have written with respect. I have not come here to judge or to call anyone out. What you'll find here are my stories — and like all stories, they carry both shadows and light.

The truth is, if you had known me in the past, you might have thought I looked angry. People even told me that once. But if you saw me now, you might repeat the same thing — only now it's not anger, it's the weight of carrying so much, the stress of creating, and the strain of becoming. And that's okay. Because the spiral doesn't ask us to appear perfect, it asks us to be honest.

This is not a book of answers. It is a book of remembrance. Each echo, each spiral, each story is offered as an invitation: to notice where your own life circles back, and to discover what waits for you on the return.

Acknowledgments

This book was not written alone. It carries the fingerprints, voices, and love of those who have walked the spiral with me. To my husband — thank you for standing beside me with patience, encouragement, and quiet acts of love that carried me through the hardest moments of writing. You are in these pages as much as I am.

To my children and grandchildren — your lives remind me why the spiral matters, why healing echoes forward, and why our stories must be told. Layla and Lilly, you are my heart's inspiration, and your laughter reminds me to keep looking for wonder.

To the readers who return with me — thank you for your willingness to circle back, to reflect, and to walk these spirals of remembrance. Your presence gives this work a life of its own.

And to the unseen guides — the synchronicities, the echoes, the gentle nudges — thank you for reminding me, again and again, that we are never alone on this path.

Chapter 1

"Life does not move in straight lines. It moves in spirals — revisiting the old until you can see it with new eyes."

The Echo of the Spiral

When most of us think of a spiral, we imagine a circle looping over and over. It can feel endless, like being trapped in the same story, repeating the same mistakes. But a true spiral is different. It doesn't only repeat — it reverberates.

What we feel in the present isn't always the wound itself, but the echo of it still moving through us. That is the nature of the spiral.

Think of the way a sound bounces in a canyon. The voice that comes back is not the same as the one that left. It has traveled, changed, stretched across distance, and returned altered. Our lives move the same way. An old insecurity, a forgotten joy, or a long-buried memory comes back — not to put us in the same place, but to show us where we are now.

The spiral brings us around to the familiar, but never in exactly the same way. A fear may return, but it does not hold us as tightly. A joy may rise again, and it may feel deeper than before. Each return carries the resonance of the past and the possibility of something new.

This is why the spiral matters. It is not punishment. It is not proof that we have failed. It is the way life teaches, layer by layer. Each echo gives us another chance to see more clearly, respond more gently, and step forward with more wisdom than we had before.

This book is about those echoes. The spiral is in the stars above us, the waters around us, the patterns within our bodies, and the stories we carry in our souls. It is in our daily struggles and in the mysteries of the universe. The spiral is the shape of return and remembrance.

Once you begin to notice it, you see it everywhere. Not as a trap, but as a path — carrying you forward, one reverberation at a time.

Had I known this truth when I was younger, I might not have fought so hard against life. I might have trusted sooner that healing doesn't mean erasing the past — it means learning the laws of life. Each return, each echo, carries wisdom I didn't know how to recognize back then.

Chapter 2

"The spiral is not a trap. It is a teacher — circling you back until you know your own strength."

The Veil and the False Self

We are born into forgetting. From the very first breath, the world begins shaping us — molding our instincts, muffling our knowing, and layering over the truth of who we are. Some call it programming. Others call it survival. But what it really is…is veiling. The veil is not just some mystical shroud between dimensions. It's the slow, quiet accumulation of ideas and identities we were never meant to wear:

- "Be good."
- "Stay quiet."
- "Don't be too much."
- "Make them proud."
- "It's dangerous to be different."

Every layer was meant to keep us safe. And for a time, maybe it did. But safety became the prison. We began to believe the mask.

I learned early what it meant to put on a mask. At home, we always had to "be good." My mother worried about appearances — what the neighbors would think — and she did whatever it took to avoid conflict outside our house. Inside, it was a different story.

My father would come home from work, collapse into his chair with a highball in hand, and drink until he passed out. My mother, furious, would scream at him and pick fights night after night. Growing up in that environment was chaotic. The only rule that seemed to matter was: *don't add to the conflict, don't make things worse, and don't be seen.*

On top of that, my mother often dressed my younger sister and me alike, almost like twins, even though we weren't. I didn't understand it at the time, but looking back, I see how it blurred the lines of who I was. I started to lose track of my own identity. I wasn't just me anymore — I was part of a "set."

These were small things on the surface, but they built the veil I would wear for years: the habit of hiding, of blending in, of playing roles that kept me safe or acceptable, even at the cost of my own truth.

The False Self: A Beautiful Lie

The false self isn't evil. It's not your enemy. It's the version of you that knew how to survive a world that didn't see your soul. It's the part that says:
- "Let me say what they want to hear."
- "Let me stay small so no one feels threatened."
- "Let me succeed so I'm finally worth something."
- "Let me help everyone else, so I don't have to face myself."

It's the carefully constructed self-made of adaptations, strategies, defenses, roles. It's the one who took the lead when the soul wasn't safe to speak. But here's the thing: **The false self mimics the soul.** It doesn't show up with devil horns. It shows up as the perfectionist, the fixer, the wise one, the healer, the good girl, the success story, the humble servant. It *seems* noble, spiritual, and productive. But it's built on fear.

Is This My Ego?

I've asked that question a thousand times. "Is this my ego talking?" "Am I just doing this for attention?" "Am I getting in the way of the truth?" "Should I stay quiet so I don't make it about me?" Let me say this plainly: **your soul is allowed to take up space.** Your truth deserves a voice. Your story is not ego. Your healing is not performance. Your light is not arrogance.

Your soul-led work is not self-promotion. Ego only gets in the way when we forget who we are.

The false self *acts spiritual*. The soul *is spirit embodied*. And you can feel the difference — not in how it looks, but in how it moves through your body. The false self creates tightness, striving, a need to be seen. The soul feels like gravity and breath and truth.

When the Veil Begins to Slip

Something always cracks first:
- The grief that won't stay buried

- The illness that forces a reckoning
- The relationship that explodes
- The emptiness that success can't fill

It's not punishment. It's the beginning of remembering. When the veil begins to lift, there is often panic. Who am I without all of this? What happens if I let it all go? Who will still love me?

Will I be lost? Will I become full of myself? These questions aren't signs that something is wrong. They are proof you are waking up. This is where the spiral begins. Not with ascension. But with disorientation.

Meeting Yourself on the Other Side

Eventually, if you keep going — not forward, but *inward* — something astonishing happens.

You meet yourself. Not the wounded version. Not the conditioned one. But the Soul — the one who was always watching, always whispering, always waiting. You realize that beneath the veil, nothing was ever missing. You were covered. You are not becoming someone new. You are remembering someone ancient.

Chapter 3

"Time does not erase. It reverberates — carrying both the ache and the wisdom forward."

Time Mirrors and Soul Memory

Time is not what we've been taught. It is not a straight line, but a spiral — looping, layering, and folding back on itself. And within that spiral, your soul is speaking to you. Not just from the past, but from *everywhere you've ever been* — and perhaps everywhere you're still becoming. When we speak of healing, we often talk about "breaking patterns." But what if these patterns aren't just wounds repeating? What if they're **messages**? What if they're **memories**? What if they are your soul — echoing through timelines — saying: "You've been here before. This time, let's walk through it awake."

The Echoes We Call Problems

You meet someone new and feel an old ache. You leave a toxic job only to recreate the same dynamic in the next. You keep saying, "I thought I already healed this." It's easy to think you're failing — repeating mistakes, attracting the same heartbreak, stuck in some karmic loop. But it's not failure. It's *recognition*. Patterns aren't always punishment. Sometimes they're *coordinates*.

Your soul is mapping itself through time. And the "problem" you're facing may not be a flaw at all — it may be a memory rising. A soul-level echo pulling you back to a fracture point, not to punish you, but to give you a chance to choose differently. To integrate what was once unbearable.

Déjà Vu, Synchronicity, and the Timeline Spiral

Have you ever felt time fold over on itself? A moment that feels too familiar...a face that stirs something ancient...a place that makes your whole body respond before your mind can catch up? These are not coincidences. They are *time mirrors* — glimpses into the spiral. Moments when the veil between timelines thin just enough for you to feel it. Sometimes they show up as:

- Recurring dates or numbers
- Repeating relationship dynamics
- Places you feel "called to" but can't explain
- Cycles that restart every few years
- Words that strike you as if you've heard them before

These are markers — invitations — reminding you: "This is the place you once forgot. Will you remember this time?"

The Moment I Saw It

For so long, I thought those strange repeat moments were proof that I was stuck — proof that I hadn't healed "enough." But one day I heard someone say: "We don't move in circles. We move in spirals." And something clicked. I realized that I wasn't repeating. I was *returning* — to the same energetic place, but from a higher place on the spiral. The lesson wasn't punishing me. It was *deepening*. Since that moment, I see it everywhere. In the podcast episodes that echo the words I just wrote in my journal. In the synchronicities that come right as I revisit something old.

In the feeling that *this moment has happened before — but now, I can respond differently.* Once you *see* the spiral, you can't un-see it. It's the structure behind awakening.

Karma or Continuum?

It's tempting to view these echoes through the lens of karma — that we're stuck repeating something we "deserve." But this book isn't about guilt. It's about *grace*. Soul memory is not about paying for the past. It's about *completing* it. You're not being punished. You're being pulled into wholeness. Each loop of the spiral is a new octave. You don't return to the same place — you return wiser. You hold more of yourself than you did the last time. You can see more clearly, respond more lovingly, and choose more freely. That is what remembering does. It doesn't erase the past. It *reorients* it.

A Spiral, Not a Cage

There is a difference between being stuck and being refined. The spiral is not a trap — think of it as a teacher. And even when you feel like you are walking through the same fire again, something is different now. Maybe it's your awareness, maybe your tenderness, or maybe it's that, this time, you know you have a choice.

You Are Not Starting Over

If you take nothing else from this chapter, let it be this: **You are not starting over.** You are starting *again* — with more wisdom, presence, and truth. The pattern you see today may be the final knot untangling. The pain you feel may be the echo's last request for your attention. The memory is not here to haunt you. It is here to remind you that you made it through once — and you can integrate it fully now. I have learned that the spiral keeps returning until you have learned that lesson.

Chapter 4

"Awakening is not a straight ascent — it's a sacred return with new eyes."

The Spiral Path of Awakening

This chapter bridges what we've just learned about soul patterns into the lived *experience* of awakening — the disorientation, initiations, and embodied transformation that unfolds when we *live* the spiral consciously. Spiritual awakening isn't what most people imagine. It doesn't start with light or bliss or transcendence. It starts with a cracking open. That moment when what used to work…doesn't. When the roles you played… stop fitting. When the old story unravels…and you don't yet know the new one. Awakening begins not in revelation, but in rupture.

Disorientation is a Sacred Signpost

We're taught that awakening is a mountaintop moment. A single flash of truth. But for most of us, it's not a peak. It's a spiral descent. This doesn't mean your life literally spirals downward — it means you revisit familiar challenges at deeper levels of truth. A deep inner unraveling. You don't ascend first. You *descend into truth*. Into your body. Into your grief. Into the parts of yourself that were never safe to feel. And it's terrifying. Because everything begins to feel unfamiliar:

The relationships you built on a version of you that no longer exists. The goals that used to excite you but now feel hollow.

The identity you clung to that begins to slip through your fingers. But this is not failure. It's not regression. It's the spiral in motion.

Spiritual Initiation is a Return to the Soul

Awakening is not about becoming enlightened. It's about becoming *intimate* with your soul. You begin to remember things you never learned. You start sensing patterns beneath your pain. You can't tolerate what you used to normalize. You feel more…and you *can't* turn it off. At first, this heightened awareness may feel like a burden. The noise, the injustice, the energy of others — it all becomes loud.

But this sensitivity is not a weakness. It's your soul speaking louder than the world for the first time in a long time. You are not breaking down. You are becoming real.

The Spiral is the Curriculum

Each loop of the spiral brings a new initiation. Not because you didn't learn the lesson — but because you're ready for a deeper one.

At first, it's personal:
- Can I set boundaries?
- Can I hear my intuition?
- Can I feel my own worth?

Then it becomes soul-based:
- Can I stay rooted when others don't understand?
- Can I speak truth without needing validation?

- Can I walk away from comfort to follow soul alignment?

Each return is not a rerun — it's a refinement. And each choice you make from soul — no matter how small — reorients your entire spiral.

Awakening is Not for the Ego

One of the hardest parts of awakening is that you can't *perform* it. You can't fake it. You can't force it. You can't bypass the parts of yourself that still ache, still doubt, still cling. In fact, those parts often get louder as you awaken — not because you're failing, but because they're finally being seen. There is no spiritual prize for being perfect. The spiral doesn't reward performance. It honors presence.

Where You Are Is Not a Mistake

Even now — if you feel lost, tired, raw, and uncertain — you are not outside the spiral.

You are *in it*. The confusion is part of it. The loneliness is part of it. The letting go of everything you thought you were is part of it. Awakening is not linear, and it is not comfortable. But it is holy. And you don't have to get it right. You just have to stay *with yourself* through the spiral.

Chapter 5

"Echoes are not punishments. They are reminders that healing deepens each time you return."

Living Symbols and Sacred Language

I didn't discover symbols in a textbook. I stumbled on them one afternoon as a child, rummaging through the "junk drawer" for something I can't even remember now. Wedged in the back was a tiny red book, no bigger than three inches by two. Its cover read something like *The Book of Everyday Omens*.

I stood there flipping through its pages, fascinated. "If you see a spider, let it live for good luck." "If you drop a knife, you'll get into an argument." Page after page of everyday signs. I studied that little booklet as if it were a secret map. And I believed it.

To this day, I still throw salt over my left shoulder when I spill it. Later, as a teenager, a strange chain letter arrived in the mail — typed, unsigned, addressed not only to me but to my sister and brother. My mother snatched it, called it nonsense, and threw it away. Not long afterward, I found myself in a situation where I was shot. That moment cemented my belief: omens and superstitions were not silly. They were warnings.

From then on, I began noticing more: angel feathers, pennies from heaven, tiny synchronicities that felt like breadcrumbs. As I grew older and studied more, my sense of symbols expanded. They became not just good or bad luck, but a language through which life itself spoke to me.

Symbols are living reminders, not decorations. They can shape the way we move through the world, and they can evolve with us — from superstition to intuition to soul language.

We've been trained to believe that logic is truth and that language must be linear to be real. But the soul has always spoken another way. Its language is layered. Nonlinear. Embodied. It speaks through:

Symbols that repeat in dreams and waking life

Images that strike your heart before your mind can explain them
Ancient patterns that stir something familiar — even if you've never studied them
A word, a shape, a number, a sign — that *feels* alive when you see it
This is sacred language. And it doesn't just carry meaning — it *remembers*. We Are Taught to Forget. From childhood, we're trained to think in straight lines. To seek "proof." To explain things clearly. To rely on what can be measured, replicated, and verified. But soul language doesn't work that way. It's intuitive. It's evocative. It's **deeply personal** — and yet somehow universal. And because of that, we're taught to dismiss it. We're told dreams are just fragments. Symbols are just metaphors. Numbers are just coincidence. That thing you felt? Just your imagination.

And so we stop listening. We forget the soul has a voice of its own.

But Then the Symbols Return

One day, a number shows up over and over again. You hear a phrase you just wrote in your journal echoed back in a podcast. A spiral, an owl, an ankh, an eclipse — keeps showing up.

And something inside you stirs. It's not just a coincidence. It's the soul speaking. It's consciousness coding. It is memory waking. Not just your memory — *collective memory*. Because symbols are how consciousness survives across time.

Why It's Returning Now

Humanity is remembering. Not all at once. Not all the same way. But we are remembering.

And one of the first things that returns in a great remembering is **symbolic literacy** — the ability to *feel* meaning without needing it explained. You know this is true, because:

- You feel it in art before you understand it
- You feel it in architecture, ancient carvings, and sacred geometry
- You feel it in dreams that make no sense — and yet linger in your body like prophecy
- You feel it when a symbol "finds you" and won't let go

This is not delusion. It's *decryption*. Your soul remembers what your intellect never learned.

Symbols Are Not Decorations — They Are Technology

The ancients didn't use symbols to be ornamental. They used them to **carry consciousness**.

Whether carved into stone, etched into tablets, or embedded in rituals, symbols were containers of frequency. They bypass the rational mind and awaken something deeper. When you encounter one of these symbols and feel a *jolt*, a stirring, a sense of "I know this" — you're not making that up. That's the memory locked in the symbol recognizing *you*.

Living the Language of the Soul

To live in alignment with your soul is to be fluent in more than just words. It is to become a reader of signs. A listener to feeling. A decoder of imagery. You begin to live symbolically — not because you're superstitious, but because you've reawakened to the reality that meaning is multilayered. A hawk doesn't just fly overhead — it brings a message. A cracked mirror doesn't just reflect — it reveals something you've been avoiding. A song, a feather, a sequence of numbers, a gut reaction — they become sacred flashes of soul communication.

You Already Know This Language

You don't have to study it. You already speak it. It's in your body. It is your blood. Your dreaming. Your remembering. The mind may argue with it. But the soul never does. If something stirs you deeply, strikes you with awe, or makes your body hum — **trust it**. Symbol is the soul's signature. It will never shout. But it will *repeat itself* until you listen.

But Not Everyone Sees It That Way

For years, I kept that part of me quiet. My husband used to call it "stupid-stition" — half-joking, half-dismissive. I'd laugh along, but inside, I'd shrink a little. It made me question myself.

Was I just being silly? Reading too much into things? But something in me *knew* it was more than that. Because long before I ever learned about energy or symbols or soul memory, I could *feel* meaning in the world around me. And when something stirs you that deeply, you don't need it to be understood by others. It's real because it's *yours*.

And once you begin to see symbols not as superstition, but as soul language…everything starts speaking again

Chapter 6

"Every spiral moment is both memory and invitation — a chance to choose differently this time."

Frequency — The Hidden Architecture of Reality

Frequency isn't always dramatic. Sometimes it's as ordinary as a family gathering. For years, during holiday get-togethers, I noticed that people's attitudes toward me were changing. They acted differently, more distant. I didn't understand why. One day, I finally said something to a family member, and they told me, "Everybody says you always look angry." I was stunned. I hadn't felt angry at all. In truth, I had started dreading those gatherings and my reluctance may have been showing on my face — but no one had ever asked.

Later, while seeing a psychologist for family counseling, the doctor looked at me and said, "Why do you look angry?" I laughed and told him I wasn't. That was the first time I'd ever heard the term *resting* b*tch face (RBF). It was such a simple moment, but it taught me a lot about frequency. People weren't reacting to my words. They were reacting to what they perceived — the energy they thought they were picking up from me. And because they never checked, an entire story built itself in the silence.

This is how frequency works. We are constantly reading signals in one another — posture, tone, expression, and subtle shifts of energy. Those signals can raise or lower the vibration of a whole room. Sometimes we're aware of it. Sometimes we're not. But our nervous systems are always listening.

19

We tend to think of reality as solid — things we can see, touch, measure. But underneath all of it, something more fundamental is moving: Vibration. Every thought, every word, every structure in the natural world — it all vibrates. It all carries frequency. And that frequency *organizes* reality. It draws in resonance and repels distortion. It builds form and carries memory. It's the blueprint beneath the visible. You are not separate from that. Your soul doesn't just live in a body. It *communicates* through frequency — subtle shifts in energy, intuition, emotion, sensation. You don't just experience life…you *emit* it.

The Forgotten Truth: You Are Tunable

We tune instruments. We tune radios. But we forget that we are instruments, too. Your body is always broadcasting. Your energy field is always receiving. Your nervous system is a living antenna. In other words, your body constantly receives and responds to subtle energy signals. When you feel "off," "in tune," "drained," "lit up," "stuck," or "clear" — that's not mood. That's **vibrational data**. And healing isn't just about fixing what's broken. It's about *re-tuning* what's distorted. Not from shame. But from remembrance.

Trauma Distorts Frequency

This is important — not to blame, but to explain. When we experience trauma — especially early or repeated trauma — our frequency gets scrambled. Our body contracts. Our energy collapses inward. We disconnect from our own natural rhythm. We go into survival patterns. We live braced. We become noisy inside, even if we seem calm on the surface. And that distortion…starts attracting distortion. Unbalanced relationships. Self-betrayal. Over-giving. Emptiness, no matter how much we accomplish. It's not a character flaw. It's a **frequency wound**.

Healing is Tuning

When we heal, we don't *add* anything to ourselves. We **release interference**. We **retune** the signal:
- Breath regulates your frequency.
- Nature harmonizes your field.
- Sound recalibrates your body.
- Stillness lets distortion rise and dissolve.
- Boundaries protect your resonance.

The more aligned your frequency becomes, the less you chase things. They begin to find you. Not because you're manifesting perfectly. But because you're becoming a *clear signal*.

You Know This Already

You can feel it when someone's energy feels "off." You know when a room is tense — even if no one says a word. You've walked into spaces that feel heavy. You've been pulled toward people who "just feel good to be around." That's not imagination. That's **resonance**. Frequency is not abstract. It's how your soul navigates reality. And now you're remembering. We are being invited to tune — not just our minds, but our *lives*. You may notice:
- A pull toward sound healing or solfeggio frequencies
- A sensitivity to music, noise, even people's voices
- A craving for silence, nature, rest

- A rejection of things that once felt "normal" but now feel jarring
- A growing awareness that your energy *matters*

This isn't hypersensitivity. It's **refinement**. You're not breaking down. You're becoming a precise instrument for soul expression.

Sound Creates Form

You don't have to take anyone's word for this. You can see it with your own eyes. There's a science called **cymatics** — the study of sound made visible. In one experiment, they placed a thin layer of sand on a flat metal plate, then played pure tones through it. At first, the sand just sat there. But as the frequency began to vibrate through the plate, something *astonishing* happened. The sand moved. It danced. It rearranged. And then it settled — not randomly, but into **perfect geometric patterns**. Flowers. Spirals. Mandalas. The higher the frequency, the more intricate the design. What struck me most when I saw the video was this: Sound — something you can't even see — created visible **order**. Vibration organized matter into beauty. And when the frequency shifted into dissonance? The pattern broke apart. The sand scattered. It wasn't broken. It was just waiting for a new tone.

That's what healing is. It's not forcing yourself into shape. It's finding your true frequency again — and letting your life re-pattern itself around it.

If frequency is the hidden architecture of reality, then water is its living bridge — the element that translates vibration into form. Every thought, every emotion, every prayer moves through it. And within us, it becomes memory made liquid.

The Water That Remembers

Science tells us that the human body is roughly seventy percent water, but numbers alone don't convey the wonder of what that means. Every thought we have, every emotion that rises and falls within us, moves through a sea of living molecules — tiny dipoles endlessly shifting, aligning, and releasing. This is not static chemistry. It is motion, rhythm, pulse. It is the physical echo of consciousness itself.

Water conducts vibration better than almost any other substance on Earth. In that way, it mirrors the function of the soul: a translator of the unseen into experience. When we speak, sing, or pray, the sound ripples through the body's inner oceans; our cells literally move with the wave. Emotion — *emovere*, to move energy — does the same. Joy, fear, gratitude, grief: each one stirs the waters differently, like weather systems on an inner sea.

Some have claimed that water can *store* memory. Perhaps not in the hard-drive sense that science demands proof for, but in a subtler way that every living being already understands. Water reflects the frequency of whatever touches it. It records not by keeping, but by *responding*. Its memory is motion. The imprint fades only when the vibration that created it dissolves. In this way, water teaches us that remembrance is not an archive — it is a continuing conversation.

Ancient cultures seemed to know this. The Egyptians spoke of *Nun*, the primordial waters from which creation rose. In

Genesis, the Spirit of God moved upon the waters before light existed. The Vedas likened consciousness to the ocean and the Self to its wave. Even our modern language preserves the intuition: we talk about "currents" of thought, "streams" of consciousness, and "depths" of feeling. Somewhere in our collective psyche, we still remember that life itself is aquatic in nature — fluid, reflective, and responsive to vibration.

When I began to sense this truth, I stopped thinking of the body as a cage and started seeing it as an instrument — one designed for resonance. We are, in essence, vessels of living water tuned to the frequency of awareness. The more coherent our internal waters, the more clearly consciousness can move through us, just as clear glass lets light pass without distortion. Healing, then, is partly a matter of purification: restoring clarity to the medium so the original signal — the song of creation — can be heard again.

Perhaps that is what the ancients meant when they spoke of the "waters of life." Not merely the element itself, but the capacity within us to flow, remember, and renew. The soul is not fixed; it moves like water, finding new channels through which to express itself. And as it does, it carries the memory of every shore it has ever touched.

Chapter 7

"The patterns you see are not flaws. They are coordinates, guiding you toward wholeness."

The Quadrinity Revisited

Growing up the way I did, worry was a constant companion. It became my normal. As an adult, the questions never stopped running through my mind: *Does my husband still love me? Is he cheating? Will he leave me?* Then there were the financial fears: *Will we have enough for food? How will I pay the bills? Will we lose our home?*

I had learned those fears as a child, watching my parents struggle and fight. And they stayed with me, lodged deep in my nervous system. Even when life was stable, the shadows of worry whispered that it could all collapse at any moment. Over time, the stress wreaked havoc on my body. I developed what doctors called a "nervous stomach." I couldn't go anywhere without planning pit stops, terrified of getting sick. After gallbladder surgery, I was prescribed medication for bile acid malabsorption, but it didn't help. I became consumed by it.

I remember one week when I went to the doctor three days in a row. On the third day, he walked into the exam room, saw me sitting there, and stopped dead in his tracks. He threw his hands in the air and said, "I don't know what to do. I can't help you anymore."

That was the moment I realized how broken my Quadrinity had become. My mind was trapped in worry. My body was breaking down. My spirit felt numb. And my soul's quiet voice — telling me to stop, to rest, to trust — was drowned out by fear.

I eventually found a new doctor, and slowly my body began to heal. I still struggle at times, but I am no longer consumed. And I've learned something important: the mind, body, spirit, and soul are not separate. They are a system. When one suffers, they all do. And when they begin to come back into balance, healing is possible. My journey showed me that the Quadrinity isn't just an idea. It's a lived reality. When one part is silenced, the others suffer. When they begin to harmonize, healing becomes possible.

The Quadrinity Revisited is where we bring all the parts of the self online as a unified instrument. This chapter connects beautifully to the theme of frequency, showing how harmony isn't about perfection — it's about integration. You are not just a body. You are not just a mind. You are not just a soul. You are not just a spirit. You are all of it. And always have been.

In *Returning to Wholeness*, we explored the idea of the **Quadrinity** — the fourfold nature of the self: **Body, Mind, Spirit, and Soul**.

You may have first encountered it through healing, through conflict, and through yearning to feel whole again. But now, you're not just *learning* the Quadrinity. You're being asked to *live* it. Not as parts…but as a single, tuned instrument.

When You're Out of Tune

Each part of you carries wisdom. Each part also carries wounds. When one part tries to lead alone, imbalance takes over:

- The **Mind** becomes noisy, controlling, or anxious
- The **Body** becomes heavy, exhausted, or reactive
- The **Spirit** floats, detached, chasing light while avoiding depth
- The **Soul** whispers...but gets drowned out by the rest

We often mistake healing for "quieting" one part — like calming the mind or grounding the body. But true healing happens when **each part is heard and harmonized.** You are not a chain of command. You are a symphony.

How the Quadrinity Sounds When Whole

Imagine this:

- The **Mind** serves as the clear translator — helping you name, plan, and choose.
- The **Body** grounds the knowing — bringing instinct, sensation, and signal.
- The **Spirit** reminds you that you're more than this — that life is guided and sacred.
- The **Soul** leads the melody — deep, ancient, unshakably true.

When these four parts are aligned, **your life becomes coherent.** Not perfect. But whole. Not effortless. But *true*. You feel what's right before you can explain it. You say no

27

without guilt. You say yes without fear. You can *feel* when something is yours — and when it isn't.

Who's Been Leading Until Now?

This is a question worth pausing over. Has it been your mind? Your body's survival instincts? A fragmented version of spirit? Have you been spiritualizing pain or bypassing truth? Have you been carrying the soul alone, while the rest of you struggles to catch up? There is no shame in this. Most of us weren't taught to live in alignment. We were taught to prioritize the mind, ignore the body, worship spirit, and neglect the soul. But the spiral brings you back. To **remember all of you**. To re-tune your Quadrinity — not as a theory, but as a living truth.

Letting the Soul Lead

The soul doesn't force the others into submission. It *orchestrates*. It listens to the body, honors the mind, welcomes spirit — and then invites them all in to a deeper coherence. This isn't a mental decision. It's a vibrational shift. You begin to live in rhythm with your truth. Your yes means yes. Your no, means no. You don't override your body. You don't spin out in thought.

You don't chase spirit to escape. You *embody* the soul…in every part of you.

You Are Not Too Much. You Are Just Unheard.

Sometimes, the disharmony isn't because something is wrong

— but because one part of you is *screaming* to be heard. The body aches. The mind spirals. The spirit loses faith. The soul grows quiet. This isn't failure. It's feedback. And the moment you begin to listen to each voice — not to control it, but to honor it — the orchestra begins to retune. The instrument remembers the song.

Chapter 8

"The body doesn't betray you. It speaks to you in echoes, waiting for you to listen."

Spirals in the Body — The Temple Within

I grew up hearing the phrase, "Your body is your temple." And for a long time, I lived by it. I was in tune with my body, able to sense the slightest shift. But after my first baby, that connection began to slip. Each pregnancy added weight, followed by endless dieting. I fell into yo-yo patterns, bouncing between control and exhaustion.

As life grew busier with kids, work, and home, I ran on autopilot. I wasn't unhealthy, but I wasn't connected either. Then everything spiraled. My stomach went haywire. I was sick all the time, afraid to leave the house. Work became nearly impossible.

A new doctor and nutritionist helped me uncover a nightshade sensitivity, and diet changes brought some relief. But when Covid hit, new challenges emerged — rapid weight gain, polycythemia, lung nodules, liver issues. At one point, I felt like my body was shutting down.

That was when I began listening again. Researched. Took supplements. Followed protocols. Slowly, I stabilized. I stopped the weight from climbing. Healing hasn't been easy — it feels more like a swing or an escalator than a straight line. But I am listening.

I've come to see my health as a spiral: each flare-up, each setback, each recovery is not failure but feedback. My body was never against me. It was echoing the stress, the imbalance, the forgetting — and inviting me back.

Your body is not just a vessel. It is a temple, a spiral, and a teacher. It remembers what the mind forgets. It will circle you back again and again until you finally hear the truth it's holding for you: that you are not separate from your body, but whole with it.

Chapter 9

"They weren't ahead of their time — they remembered something we forgot."

Visionary Thinkers and the Continuum of Consciousness

My journey into spirituality didn't begin with ancient texts or academic study. It began in the middle of a crisis. During Covid, while the world slowed down, my life sped up. I was still driving the long, empty roads to work, handling the personal affairs of my boss whose brilliant mind was slowly being taken by dementia.

Each drive felt heavy. The world outside felt uncertain. Inside, I was exhausted and anxious, wishing I could stay home where it felt safe. To make the drive bearable, I began turning on YouTube — meditation music, self-help videos, conversations with people who seemed to hold pieces of wisdom.

Not every video was trustworthy. I learned quickly to be discerning, to research, to check sources before believing anything. But some of what I heard began to change me. It wasn't entirely new — more like echoes of something I'd sensed but couldn't articulate.

I remember listening to guided meditations at night when I couldn't sleep, lying awake in the dark. Slowly, my body began to rest again. Slowly, my mind began to soften. My spiritual journey had begun long before, but in that season it took root and began to blossom. The continuum of consciousness isn't about idolizing figures from history or influencers of today. It's about recognizing that wisdom flows through time and shows up where it's needed. The spiral brings us the voices and teachings we're ready for — and asks us to test, to discern, and to integrate them into our own lives.

That's what visionaries do. Whether they lived centuries ago or speak today on a platform, they remind us of truths we've forgotten. They don't give us answers; they help us remember our own.

We often describe mystics, inventors, and consciousness pioneers as "ahead of their time." But what if they weren't ahead at all? What if they were simply *tuned* to a wider bandwidth — remembering what most had forgotten? These visionaries didn't invent new truths. They *accessed* the continuum — the thread of consciousness that's always been here, waiting for someone to listen. They reminded us — through science, philosophy, healing, and energy — that the nature of reality is not fixed, and neither are we.

Memory Is Not Just Personal — It's Planetary

As your spiral deepens, you begin to realize: your awakening is not isolated. It's not just about healing your own wounds. It's about plugging back into the **field** — the shared memory bank of consciousness. And through that field, you begin to resonate with others across time — those whose thoughts, inventions, writings, and experiments mirror what your soul already knows.

This is where thinkers like **David Bohm, Joseph Murphy, Rudolf Steiner, and Nikola Tesla** come in — not as authorities, but as *fellow rememberers.*

Joseph Murphy — Thought as Frequency, Prayer as Activation

Murphy taught that **the subconscious mind responds to frequency**, not force. That prayer isn't begging — it's *aligning.* He called it scientific prayer:

- Not repetition
- Not pleading

But *impressing* your subconscious with a clear inner picture, so powerfully felt that reality begins to mold around it.

He believed that the Divine wasn't "out there," but woven into our very *thinking.* In a way, he was describing **quantum entrainment** before it had a name — showing that our beliefs are not private. They *broadcast.* They co-create.

David Bohm — The Implicate Order and the Undivided Whole

Bohm, a theoretical physicist and student of Einstein, proposed something radical: that the universe is not made of separate things...but of **undivided wholeness in flowing movement.**

He called it the **Implicate Order** — an unseen field beneath what we call reality. Everything we experience, he said, unfolds from this hidden order like a hologram — whole in every part. This isn't far from what mystics have always said:

- That we are not disconnected.
- That all is within all.
- That separation is the illusion, not unity.

When I first heard Bohm's theory, I felt it more than understood it. It wasn't just science. It was *soul confirmation.*

Rudolf Steiner — Etheric Forces and the Memory of the Cosmos

Steiner, philosopher and founder of anthroposophy, spoke of the **etheric body** — the energetic counterpart to the physical body. He taught that we carry not just genetic memory, but **cosmic memory**. That the stars, the planets, the movements of the heavens were part of our inner blueprint. That children are not blank slates, but *souls with stories* returning.

Steiner saw education, agriculture, medicine — all of it — as opportunities to align with the spiritual forces moving through creation. He was bridging soul and system. Matter and meaning. Structure and spirit.

Nikola Tesla — Frequency, Vibration, and the Living Current

Tesla once said, *"If you want to find the secrets of the universe, think in terms of energy, frequency, and vibration."* Long before quantum models, Tesla was speaking the language of the soul — through electricity. He believed that free energy pulsed all around us — and could be harnessed not just for power, but for healing, consciousness, and communication. The mainstream dismissed him. But to those walking the spiral, his words now ring like prophecy. Tesla didn't just invent. He *tuned in* — and tried to bring the invisible into form.

They Remembered. So Do You.

These thinkers weren't gods or gurus. They were *translators*. They found language for the things most people only felt. And now...you're doing the same. You are no longer just absorbing ideas. You're recognizing them and feeling the resonance. Waking up your own internal memory bank — not to mimic them, but to **remember what they remembered**, in your own way. This is the continuum. And your soul is part of it.

Chapter 10

"You are never starting over. You are always starting again — with more wisdom than before."

Anchoring Soul Truth in the Physical World

Soul-truth isn't just something we remember — it's something we live, moment by moment, choice by choice. It's one thing to awaken. It's another to *walk* as the awakened self — in conversations, in conflict, in chaos, in money, in family, in your daily rhythm. Spiritual remembering can feel profound when you're alone in meditation, journaling, or listening to a podcast that speaks directly to your soul. But what happens when:

- Someone interrupts your peace?
- A bill is due and your nervous system panics?
- An old relationship dynamic tries to hook you back in?
- You want to say no, but the pattern says yes?

This is where truth gets **anchored** — or lost. Not in ideas. In *embodiment*.

Integration Is a Daily Practice

You don't "graduate" from healing and awakening. You *apply it*, again and again, as life offers you moments to choose:

- Do I respond from my old self or my soul self?
- Do I shrink to keep the peace, or speak from truth?
- Do I abandon myself again, or stay with my body this time?

These aren't tests. They're *recalibrations*. Each moment you choose alignment, even imperfectly, you make your soul *more real* in this world. Not in theory. In form.

It's Supposed to Be Awkward at First

Walking your soul truth can feel clunky. Disorienting. Lonely. You might:

- Outgrow conversations you once loved
- Notice you're more sensitive to noise, clutter, or surface energy
- Struggle to explain what you're feeling because language hasn't caught up
- Second-guess your boundaries
- Feel the urge to *retreat*, even as you're being called to *show up*

This doesn't mean you're off track. It means your **external life is adjusting to your internal frequency.** And that takes time.

Alignment Over Approval

This is one of the hardest parts of anchoring soul truth: You might lose things that once defined you:

- Roles
- Relationships
- Titles
- Reputations
- Old coping patterns

And in their place…is:
- Space.
- Stillness
- Unknown.

It's terrifying — until you realize: You didn't lose yourself. You *found* yourself. And now, you're building a life that doesn't just look good…It *feels like home.*

What Does Anchoring Look Like?

It's not all big declarations or leaving your job overnight. Sometimes, anchoring looks like:
- Saying no without over-explaining
- Turning your phone off to breathe
- Not reacting to bait
- Trusting your body over your brain
- Creating beauty in your home, just because it lifts your frequency
- Choosing nourishment over numbing

It's not dramatic. It's *devotional.* Anchoring is the moment your inner truth meets your outer world — and refuses to betray itself.

Soul Truth Changes Everything (And That's the Point)

As you anchor, you'll begin to notice:
- You no longer tolerate energetic misalignment
- You crave authenticity over comfort

- You magnetize new opportunities that match your inner state
- You no longer need to be "understood" — just to be real

This isn't about becoming someone new. It's about *living as who you've always been.* Not just in vision. But in the messy, sacred details of daily life.

"Where in my life am I still hiding my truth?"

I am still learning that I am not hiding a truth because I am deceptive, but because I am afraid it might be ego. And that's what so many people silently wrestle with on the spiritual path — especially women, especially the sensitive and sincere.

Reflection

Maybe it's not about hiding my truth. Maybe it's about learning to *trust* that my truth isn't ego-driven just because it's strong, clear, or different from what others expect. What if my soul voice is *bigger* than I let it be? What if what I call ego…is actually truth rising?

Journal Prompt

Where in my life do I silence myself out of fear that I'll be "too much"?
What would it feel like to let my soul lead — even if it's misunderstood?

Chapter 11

"Old wounds return not to destroy you, but to show you where you are ready to rise."

The Spiral of the Everyday

The spiral isn't only found in galaxies, temples, or ancient carvings. It shows up in the ordinary, messy places of life — in the emotions we wrestle with, in the words we remember, and in the relationships that both bless and challenge us.

For me, one of the clearest spirals has been jealousy. It didn't arrive once and disappear. It circled through my life again and again, sometimes so strong it threatened to undo everything I loved. The roots were planted early. As a child and teenager, I often felt judged by appearances. At one stage, I was "too much" of one thing, and later I was "too much" of another. Just as I began to wonder if maybe I was worth noticing, someone close to me warned that the sudden attention I was receiving wasn't about *me* at all — only about what I looked like. Those words lodged deep. They whispered: *You will never be valued for who you really are.*

Over time, those whispers grew into a spiral of jealousy. Whenever someone came close, the fear circled back: *What if I'm not enough? What if someone else is more?* It made me cling too tightly, mistrust what was good, or sabotage what might have been steady and kind. For years, I thought jealousy was proof that others couldn't be trusted. But in truth, it was the echo of an old wound still moving through me. For so long, I believed I was failing. No one ever explained that life itself

41

moves this way — that wounds return as teachers, that patterns repeat until they are healed. If I had known that this was one of life's laws, I might have met myself with more compassion instead of shame.

That's what spirals do. They don't just repeat the same experience — they reverberate, carrying the resonance of what has not yet been healed. Each time jealousy returned, it wasn't punishment. It was an invitation. At first, I couldn't see that. The spiral swallowed me whole. But with time, I began to notice: the intensity was shorter, the grip was looser. I realized the jealousy wasn't about other people. It was about the part of me that still longed to be chosen, safe, and seen.

The spiral taught me that growth doesn't mean the wound disappears. It means that each time it circles back, I have a chance to meet it differently. To breathe instead of react. To pause instead of collapse. To tell myself a truer story: *I am not unworthy. I am not in danger. I am enough.*

That is the hidden gift of the everyday spiral. It shows up in our kitchens and our bedrooms, in conversations and in silences. It shows us that healing is not linear. It is layered, revisited, refined. And the echoes of our old stories are not proof that we are failing. They are proof that we are remembering.

Reflection

Think of a pattern that still circles back in your life — an emotion, a reaction, or a belief. How does it usually appear? What might it be echoing from your past?

Affirmation

Each time the spiral returns, I have the chance to rise a little higher.

Journal Prompt

What emotion or reaction in my life feels like a spiral?
How has it changed over time — do I recover faster, respond
differently, or see it more clearly now?
What truth can I remind myself of when this spiral returns?

Chapter 12

"The patterns you see are not flaws. They are coordinates, guiding you toward wholeness."

The New Earth and Spiral Citizenship

There's a quiet revolution happening. Not one with headlines or grand declarations, but one that's happening inside hearts and bodies — one choice at a time. People are waking up. Not all at once, and not all the same way. But the spiral is calling, and more souls are hearing it.

The Earth is shifting, too. Not just in weather patterns and pole movements — but in **frequency**.

We're not just remembering who we are. We're beginning to ask: *What kind of world do we want to live in — and how do we create it without recreating the old one?*

The Old Earth Was Built on Fear

The systems we were born into — education, government, media, and religion — were built on control. Scarcity. Hierarchy. Image. Survival. Ego dressed in authority. We were taught:
- Success means self-abandonment
- Power means domination
- Truth must be proven
- Intuition is unreliable
- Worth must be earned

And we internalized it. We tried to play by the rules. Until our souls began to ache. Because the old Earth never made space for the soul.

Spiral Citizenship

My connection to the Earth began when I was very young. I remember lying in bed during summer nights with the windows open, staring out at the trees, the grass, and the flowers. The sounds of nature would drift in, calming me. When I did go outside, I often found myself sitting on the neighbor's lawn or tucked away in the weeds, simply watching and listening.

I was allergic to poison sumac, but I didn't know it at the time. Looking back, I laugh at how often I must have been sitting right in it, picking at the plants, only to end up at the doctor's office for cortisone shots. Even then, I couldn't stay away from nature. Something in me felt at home there.

As an adult, that love hasn't left me. This past summer, I created a small "Zen" garden — a place to sit, reflect, and be with the Earth. It's where I feel most able to listen, not just to myself but to the planet. As a child, the Earth felt calm to me. Now, when I sit in my garden, I sometimes sense her chaotic vibrations. I can feel that something is unsettled. And I find myself hoping that, whatever she is moving through, she can heal before something more serious happens.

For me, this is what it means to live as a citizen of the spiral: to care for the Earth not as an idea, but as a living being who speaks to us — if we are willing to listen.

45

The New Earth isn't a place. It's a **frequency**. And to live there, is to walk the spiral — not as an escape from the world, but as a new kind of *citizenship* within it.

A **spiral citizen:**
- Knows that truth is living not fixed
- Responds instead of reacts
- Doesn't strive to rise above pain, but meets it with presence
- Sees community as sacred, not transactional
- Listens for the soul beneath the story
- Trusts cycles more than outcomes

They are builders — not of empires, but of resonance. And they anchor a New Earth not by preaching it — but by *living it*, in every interaction.

5D Is Not a Place — It's a State of Frequency

We hear the term "5D" more and more now — often spoken of like a destination or reward. But it's not a zip code or a spiritual achievement. It's a **shift in perception and embodiment**.

To live in 5D is to:
- Be present in the body *and* aware of the field
- Act from alignment, not conditioning
- Create from coherence, not scarcity
- Feel deeply without becoming overwhelmed
- Trust intuition as equal to intellect

The 5D reality doesn't erase difficulty. It **transforms your relationship to it**. You stop seeing problems as punishments — and start seeing them as prompts for recalibration.

We're Not Waiting for a New Earth — We're Becoming It

You don't need permission. You don't need credentials. You don't need anyone to validate that what you feel is real. The New Earth isn't being given to us. It's being *birthed through us* — through our presence, our remembrance, our integration. Each soul who heals becomes a frequency holder. Each person who speaks truth anchors a new pattern. Each time you respond from love instead of fear, you ripple something into the collective field. You may never see the effect. But the field knows. The Earth knows. And your soul *absolutely* knows.

The Spiral Never Ends — But It Deepens

You are not finished. This isn't a conclusion. It's a convergence. The personal, the planetary, and the cosmic are all spiraling together now. And as you walk your path — through the quiet, the mess, the miracles — know this: You are not behind. You are not broken. You are not alone. You are becoming. And you are *becoming something ancient.*

If you take nothing else from this book, let it be this: you are not broken. You are learning the very laws of life — the truths no one may have told you, but which the spiral has always held. And every echo you feel is proof, not of failure, but of your becoming.

Chapter 13

"You are not starting over. You are starting again — with more
wisdom, presence, and truth."

The Spiral of Time

For much of my life, I called them patterns. Only later did I
understand them as spirals. Relationships were the clearest
place I saw them. Again and again, they circled back to the
same result. Looking back, I see how much of that came from
me — from the ways I would self-sabotage, from the jealousy,
worry, and fear I carried.

One of the reasons I married my current husband is because
he was so different from my "norm." He didn't fit the old
pattern. Even then, my shadows tried to circle back, pulling
me toward the familiar spiral of mistrust. But he loved me
enough to work with me through it. Thirty-two years later, he
still does.

The spiral of time didn't just show up in relationships. It
appeared at work too. I've always held long-term jobs, but
even there I would find myself in the same dynamics repeating
— feeling undervalued, carrying too much, doubting myself.
Once I began to see the spiral, I could work through those
situations instead of collapsing into them.

That's the gift of the spiral of time. It doesn't erase our
patterns — it brings them back until we can meet them
differently. It takes a lot of getting to know yourself, not only
the shadows but also the light. To recognize not just where

you sabotage yourself, but where you are good, loving, and deserving. When I began to see that truth — that I was not only loved, but worthy of love — something in the spiral began to heal.

We've been taught to picture time as a straight line. Past behind us. Present in the middle. Future stretching out ahead. But the soul knows something different: time does not move in a line. It moves in spirals.

You've felt this before. That moment of déjà vu when a place feels uncannily familiar, even though you know you've never been there. The same type of relationship dynamic showing up years later, only with different faces. A historical event unfolding in the present that looks eerily like something you studied in school. These are not random repetitions. They are echoes.

The spiral of time means that nothing truly disappears. Experiences reverberate forward, carrying their imprint into new cycles. What looks like a repeat is really a return — a chance to meet the old with new awareness.

Echoes in History

History itself reveals the spiral. Empires rise and fall, often for the same reasons: greed, division, corruption, the neglect of the soul. Yet each collapse is not identical. Each leaves behind lessons, records, and memories that shape what comes next. The fall of Rome doesn't look exactly like the unraveling of modern nations, but the echoes are there — patterns repeating, reverberating, and asking if we will choose differently this time.

When the spiral of time loops back, it doesn't condemn us. It invites us. It says: *You've been here before. Will you respond the same way, or will you rise into a new octave of understanding?*

Echoes in the Soul

On a personal level, the spiral of time feels like patterns we can't seem to escape. You leave one relationship only to find yourself in another that mirrors it. You outgrow one job, only to recreate the same stress in the next. At first, it feels like failure. But what if these aren't mistakes? What if they're coordinates?

The spiral teaches us that our soul remembers what our mind has forgotten. It brings us back to unfinished places, not as punishment, but as completion. A wound that once broke you may return, but now you have more wisdom, more strength, and more compassion than you did before. This is how time heals — not by erasing, but by returning with new eyes.

Time as Continuum

Ancient cultures often saw time as cyclical, not linear. The Mayan calendar, for instance, was not just about marking days. It mapped cosmic cycles — waves of creation and renewal. Hindu philosophy speaks of Yugas, vast cycles of ages that repeat, but each time with a different character. Even our own seasons remind us: spring, summer, autumn, winter — and then spring again. Yet each spring is not the same as the last. Each carries echoes of the past, layered with the freshness of the present. The spiral of time means we are never starting over. We are always starting again — wiser, more whole, and more awake than before.

Living with Time as Spiral

If you begin to see your life through the spiral of time, the frustration of repetition softens. You stop asking, *why am I back here again?* And instead ask, *what new awareness do I bring to this familiar place?* Time is not your enemy. It is your companion. It brings you back, not to trap you, but to refine you. To show you that what echoes today is not failure — it is memory calling you home.

Reflection

Think of a moment that felt like history repeating — in your own life or in the world. What was familiar about it? What was different this time?

Affirmation

I am not repeating the past. I am returning with new eyes, new strength, and new wisdom.

Journal Prompts

- What experiences in my life feel like they've circled back?
- How do I know I am meeting them from a higher place on the spiral?
- What lesson might time itself be trying to teach me?

Chapter 14

"Every return is not proof of failure, but of becoming — layer by layer, echo by echo."

The Spiral as Gateway

Some gateways arrive quietly. Others break you open. One of mine came through my daughter.

When she was little, I thought we had built the perfect little family. My husband and I didn't drink, we tried to keep our disagreements away from the children, and I wanted to give them a better life than the one I'd grown up with. But the stress of work and the weight of old patterns followed me anyway. I ended up in therapy and on medication for anxiety.

One Thanksgiving, when my daughter was in grade school, she told her class what she was grateful for. Later I asked her, and she said, *"That my mommy is on medicine and she doesn't holler anymore."* That moment pierced me. I realized that, despite my best efforts, the spiral had carried me back to what I had sworn I wouldn't repeat. I was becoming my mother. Even my father, before he died, once looked at me and said, *"You're just like your mother was. She was a screecher."*

I tried to change. I tried to soften. And my daughter grew into a strong, independent, deeply empathic woman — qualities she carried in her own right. She once sat in a McDonald's and cried when she saw an elderly man eating alone, because she could feel his loneliness.

But the gateway came later, when she almost died. A simple medical procedure turned complicated, and she never told us until afterward. She said she didn't want to worry us. In that moment, I realized how much I must have interfered in the past, how much I had tried to control out of love. Maybe that was why she kept this from me.

That was the threshold. The spiral had brought me to a place where I had no choice but to step back. To trust her, not as my child but as the woman and mother she had become. I am grateful every day that she is still here — for her girls, for her family, for us. And I carry the lesson: sometimes the spiral leads us to a gateway we never wanted to face, but crossing it changes everything.

Every initiation begins with a threshold. There is life as you have known it, and then there is the crossing — the step into something you cannot yet name. For many, the spiral is that threshold. It is the gateway between what was and what is becoming.

Threshold Experiences

Most people know what it feels like to stand at the edge of themselves. Sometimes it comes through a near-death experience. Sometimes through grief that cracks the heart open. Sometimes through altered states, prayer, or deep meditation. In those moments, the ordinary dissolves and you glimpse something more — a vastness you cannot explain, but cannot deny.

The spiral is always there in these threshold moments. You feel it in the dizziness of surrender, the circling back of memory, the strange sense that you have been here before and will be here again. The spiral carries you through the doorway.

The Spiral of Initiation

In ancient traditions, initiation was not about achievement — It was about transformation. You entered as one version of yourself and returned as another. Shamans, mystics, and wisdom keepers often described their journeys as spiral paths: descending into the underworld, circling through visions, then ascending into new life.

The spiral was the map. The descent was not regression — it was necessary. The circling was not delay — it was integration. The ascent was not escape — it was embodiment. To walk the spiral was to walk the gateway itself.

Everyday Gateways

Not all initiations are dramatic. Some are quiet thresholds in daily life. The moment you finally set a boundary you once thought impossible. The day you realize you no longer believe the story that used to control you. The quiet shift when you stop abandoning yourself. These are gateways, too — small spirals of remembrance that change everything.

Why the Spiral Is the Gateway

The spiral carries us back, but never to the same place. Each return is a doorway into deeper presence, truer alignment, and wider awareness. Without the spiral, we would be trapped in repetition. With the spiral, every echo becomes a passageway.

To walk the spiral is to accept that initiation is not a single moment, but a living process. You don't cross the gateway once. You cross it again and again — each time with more clarity, more compassion, and more courage.

Reflection

What thresholds have you walked in your own life? How did the experience change you?

Affirmation

Every return is a gateway. I cross each threshold with new strength and deeper truth.

Journal Prompts

- What moments in my life have felt like gateways?
- How did I enter — and how did I return?
- What spiral am I standing at the threshold of now?

Chapter 15

"The spiral is not just a shape. It's the signature of creation."

Spirals in Nature and the Cosmos

Spirals don't only appear in shells or galaxies. They show up in the everyday ways we connect with beauty. I've never thought of myself as an artist, but when I doodle, I almost always find myself drawing spirals, flowers, trees, or the sun. My hand seems to remember the pattern even when my mind isn't paying attention.

Every day, I'm awed by nature. By life itself. How could so much beauty exist without God/Source/Creator behind it? Sometimes I imagine heaven as one vast garden — a place to simply sit forever, listening to birds, crickets, rain, and breeze. Even now, I create moments to return to that wonder. I track eclipses, meteor showers, and other celestial events, planning evenings to watch them. Once, my family even drove four hours to my daughter's home just to be in the path of totality for a solar eclipse. Standing there, seeing the day turn to night, I felt the spiral of the cosmos in motion — both vast and intimate, echoing the same patterns I doodled in the margins of notebooks as a child.

These are not random experiences. They are reminders that the spiral is everywhere, inviting us back into wonder.

Before you ever heard the word "spiral," your body already knew it. Long before language or belief systems, the spiral was speaking — in the curl of waves, the reach of galaxies, the unfurling of a fern. It's not just a visual pattern. It's the *form that life prefers*. And maybe…the form your soul remembers.

The Spiral is Everywhere

In nature, the spiral shows up over and over again — not as decoration, but as a design of **efficiency, growth, and expansion**. You can find it in:

- **Galaxies** swirling with stars
- **Hurricanes** moving over oceans
- **Snail shells** coiled in perfect sequence
- **Ferns** uncurling in Fibonacci spirals
- **Seeds** arranged on a sunflower
- **DNA** winding in its double helix
- Even in the **cochlea** of your ear — the part that lets you *hear*

It's in the vastness of space and the softness of your own biology. The spiral holds life together. And it moves life *forward*.

The Fibonacci Sequence and Sacred Geometry

At the heart of the spiral is a mathematical principle: the **Fibonacci sequence** — a series of numbers (1, 1, 2, 3, 5, 8, 13…) where each number is the sum of the two before it. When plotted visually, this creates the familiar **golden spiral**. This spiral isn't rigid — it **expands outward**, creating ever-wider arcs, just like consciousness itself. Ancient architects and mystics knew this.

That's why we find the golden ratio in:

- Egyptian pyramids
- Greek temples
- Gothic cathedrals
- da Vinci's artwork
- The layout of sacred sites

The spiral was never random. It was sacred structure.

Why You Doodle Spirals

I used to draw spirals without thinking. They'd show up in the margins of notebooks, the backs of receipts, scratched into the steam on the shower glass. I thought it was just mindless — a default shape my hand liked. But now I wonder…What if it wasn't mindless? What If it was *remembering?* Science shows the spiral is a universal growth pattern. My doodling was another way my body mirrored that truth. Maybe you've done it too — absentminded spirals on paper. Maybe that was your body's way of tracing your path back to yourself.

The Spiral is How Energy Moves

The spiral is more than shape — it's *motion*: Tornadoes spiral. Water drains in a spiral. Galaxies rotate .Kundalini energy rises like a coiling spiral up the spine. Even your **chakra system**, if you look closely, is shown as spinning wheels — spirals of energy opening and aligning as you heal and remember. The spiral is how life flows. It doesn't charge in a straight line. It returns, expands, deepens. And you do too.

Reflection from the Spiral

"I thought I was just doodling." There's something I do when my mind is tired — not thinking, not working, just drifting. I let my hand move freely on the page. And almost every time, without planning it, I draw spirals. Little loops. Big curls. Open, slow, wide-turning spirals. They come out of me like breath. I never thought much of it. It felt automatic. Mindless. But now I see it differently. Maybe I wasn't doodling for distraction. Maybe I was tracing a memory. Maybe my hand was doing what my soul never stopped doing — **remembering the path**. The spiral is how I move, how I come back to myself, how I deepen into truth. It's not just a shape anymore. It's a *signature* — of something ancient in me still turning, still whispering, still becoming.

Chapter 16

"Before there were words for God, there were spirals carved in stone."

Ancient Spirals, Triskele, and the Sacred Return

The first time I saw the triskele, it reminded me of waves. Three curling currents, circling into one. For me, it didn't feel like an abstract symbol — it felt like the ocean.

I've always had reverence for the sea. I love the beach, love sitting on the sand to watch and listen to the waves. There's nothing more calming than that rhythm. And yet, I don't swim. The few times I've tried, I sink like a stone. I never go deeper than my knees.

Part of me laughs at that. Another part of me wonders if I drowned in a past life, because the ocean carries both peace and fear for me. Its power is undeniable. It humbles me. It demands respect.

That is the impression I carry when I look at the triskele: the endless motion of something greater than me, beautiful and dangerous all at once. A reminder that the spiral isn't only a pattern carved in stone. It's the eternal movement of life itself — waves rising, falling, returning.

Long before books, before temples, before religion — people were carving spirals into stone. They weren't decorating. They were **remembering**. Across the world — in caves, on burial mounds, in sacred sites — spirals appear again and again. Sometimes alone. Sometimes in pairs. Sometimes in **threes**.

The spiral wasn't a trend. It was a **map**. A symbol of return. A symbol of motion. A symbol of something *the soul knew to be true.*

The Spiral as Sacred Movement

In many ancient cultures, the spiral represented:
- Life, death, and rebirth
- The path of the sun
- The journey between worlds or dimensions
- The unfolding of inner and outer awareness at sites like: **Newgrange** in Ireland (older than Stonehenge), triple spirals mark passage tombs aligned with the winter solstice sunrise.

Malta's Hypogeum shows spiral patterns in a subterranean temple tuned to acoustic resonance.

Native American petroglyphs often include spirals near ceremonial spaces, believed to represent **spirit journeys** or portals.

These weren't just aesthetic. They were **activated symbols** — codes. By codes, I mean symbols carrying meaning and memory across generations.

The Triskele's Deeper Meaning

One of the most powerful spiral symbols is the **triskele** (or triskelion) — a triple-armed spiral often associated with the Celts. Each arm spirals outward from a common center, symbolizing:
- Mind, Body, Spirit

- Past, Present, Future
- Birth, Life, Death
- Or Land, Sea, Sky

It is a symbol of balance and motion. Of the soul in perpetual transformation. Of **cyclical consciousness** — where nothing is lost, only changed. When you look at the triskele, you don't just see three paths. You feel something *returning*. It stirs that deep knowing: "I've been here before — but I'm not the same." "This is the same path — but I'm walking it wiser now." That's spiral truth. That's evolution.

The Spiral's Misuse — and Reclaiming It

Yes. And that must be said. In recent decades, certain spiral motifs — especially **tight, continuous spirals** — have been coopted and used as **coded symbols for harm**, including by those involved in child exploitation. These are real and documented misuses. And they are **grotesque distortions** of something sacred. But here's what matters: The spiral existed *long before* it was ever corrupted. The spiral belongs to **life**, not to predators. Just because something was stolen doesn't mean we stop using it — we **reclaim** it. To abandon the spiral is to abandon a part of our soul language. To reclaim it is to **heal the symbol itself.** By remembering the spiral's sacred roots, you restore it to truth.

Spirals Are How We Return — But Changed

Ancient wisdom never moved in straight lines. It honored cycles. It honored decay and regeneration. It knew that to go forward, you often had to *circle back* — with new eyes, a new heart, a deeper knowing. That's what the ancients carved in stone. And that's what you're carving into your life now. Each time you return to an old lesson with more compassion…Each time you revisit an old story from a new level of awareness…Each time you say, "I've been here before, but something's different"…You are living the triskele. You are becoming spiral wisdom in motion.

Chapter 17

"Consciousness doesn't climb a ladder. It moves in spirals."

Spiral Dynamics and Conscious Evolution

The spiral doesn't only show up in big life lessons. It circles back in the smallest of moments, right in the middle of ordinary days.

Not long ago, I had one of those days where I was juggling everything — laundry, sewing, working on the business. By the time my husband got home, I was already stretched thin. He sat down and began sorting through his coins, and I felt a wave of frustration. I wished he would have helped with dinner, but instead of asking, I stayed silent and let the resentment build.

Later that night, he offered to make the bed. I was grateful, until I came upstairs and saw that my side — with its complicated pillow system — had been left undone. I was exhausted. Instead of brushing it off, I let that state of fatigue and emotion spiral me into hurt.

That's my everyday spiral. I take on too many tasks, don't ask for help, and then lash out when I feel unseen. I'm learning to recognize it now, to pause before the echo takes over. I'm learning that sometimes the spiral is not about others at all. It's about my own patterns, and the choice to step out of them — even in the smallest of moments.

What is Spiral Dynamics?

Spiral Dynamics is a framework developed by Clare Graves (and later expanded by Beck & Cowan) that maps the evolution of human consciousness — in individuals, cultures, and systems.

Rather than seeing human growth as a straight line — from primitive to advanced, from worse to better — it presents a **spiral of expanding perspectives**. Each turn of the spiral represents a new way of thinking, a new set of values, and a new understanding of what life means.

Each layer of the spiral is called a **vMEME** (short for "value meme") — a worldview, a lens through which reality is interpreted. It carries a distinct pattern of beliefs, motivations, and behaviors that arise in response to life conditions.

And here's the beauty: no level is "higher" or "better." Each one emerges to meet the needs of its time, both personally and collectively. Growth isn't about climbing a ladder — it's about evolving through spirals of awareness.

The Core Levels (Simplified)

Let's lightly touch on a few of the most recognized levels. (These are not boxes — they are **experiences**, sometimes overlapping.)

- **Beige**: Survival-focused. Instinct, food, shelter. (Infancy, crisis states)
- **Red**: Power-driven. Might makes right. Control, tribal dominance.

- **Blue**: Order and rules. Religion, structure, tradition, authority.
- **Orange**: Achievement and success. Science, capitalism, rationality.
- **Green**: Equality, community, emotional intelligence, pluralism.
- **Yellow**: Systemic thinking. Integration of opposites. Flexible awareness.
- **Turquoise**: Holistic unity. Spiritual awareness, living systems consciousness.

Many people cycle through multiple levels over a lifetime. Some never move beyond one. Some spiral up, then down, then back again — as needed. It's not linear. It's alive.

Spiral Dynamics Meets the Soul

You might feel this spiral inside you — not as a theory, but as lived experience:
- Times when survival ruled your choices (Beige)
- Times you rebelled or controlled (Red)
- Times you clung to rules to feel safe (Blue)
- Times you chased success and logic (Orange)
- Times your heart cracked open to justice and empathy (Green)
- Times you glimpsed *all* of it — and began weaving it together (Yellow/Turquoise)

The spiral of consciousness is not a race. It's a **rhythm** — and your soul has danced to it across lifetimes.

Why It Matters Now

As the Earth shifts, more people are feeling internal dissonance — like the old stories don't fit, the old structures feel hollow, and something *deeper* is trying to emerge. That's not regression.

That's evolution. You're not going crazy. You're outgrowing containers that no longer fit your frequency. And Spiral Dynamics offers one lens — one map — to show you that this growth has *always* been part of the plan.

Chapter 18

"Light is not just illumination. It is information."

The Light Remembers

Some spirals live deeper than memory. They live in the soul. I've always loved the ocean. Its sound calms me, its rhythm soothes me. Yet I've never wanted to live near it, and I've never learned to swim. When I go in, I sink like a stone. There's a part of me that wonders if, in another time, I drowned there. Whether it's fear, intuition, or a memory older than this life, I don't know. But my reverence for the ocean remains — its peace, its power, its warning.

I've felt similar pulls in other places. Gettysburg is one of them. We've visited several times with friends, even doing some ghost hunting. There are areas — the battlefield, the Witness Tree — that draw me in a way I can't explain. Not like déjà vu, but like recognition without words.

And then there's the déjà vu itself. I've experienced it many times, sometimes followed by dizzy spells, as if I've momentarily stepped into an echo of myself. I've never been able to link those episodes to a specific spiral, but they remind me that time isn't as linear as it seems.

I don't have all the answers. But I've learned to trust these pulls as part of the soul's spiral return — not to romanticize them, but to listen. The spiral doesn't only circle us back to lessons from this life. It can also carry echoes from lifetimes we don't remember, guiding us toward wholeness one return at a time.

In 2023, physicists published something extraordinary. Using a complex setup involving entangled photons and a quantum computing model, they measured light behaving across **37 dimensions** of space. Not 3. Not 4. **Thirty-seven.**

For most people, this made little sense. But for some of us — it felt like a cosmic confirmation. What we've sensed for years, whispered in dreams or echoed in mystical texts, suddenly had scientific echoes: Consciousness is not confined. Memory is not linear. Light is multidimensional — and so are we.

The Photon Knows

Photons are packets of light — the smallest measurable unit of electromagnetic energy. But in many ancient and esoteric traditions, light is more than a wave or a particle. It's **a carrier of memory.** A messenger. A builder of reality.

This experiment — exploring light in 37 dimensions — didn't just push physics forward. It pushed the veil a little thinner. It made visible what mystics and initiates have long taught: Light is a bridge between spirit and matter. Light remembers what we forget.

Light as a Spiral of Consciousness

When light travels, it doesn't move in a perfect straight line. It can twist, oscillate, spiral — even entangle across time and space. Some theorists believe that light might actually encode **experience** the way DNA encodes biological instruction.

So what if:

- The light that touches your skin carries imprints from stars born eons ago?
- The light in your cells remembers things your conscious mind cannot?
- You — made of stardust — are also made of **remembered light**?

In that way, your soul is not just energy. It is organized light. It is encoded memory.

From Science to Soul

You don't need a lab to know what this experiment confirmed. You've *felt* those moments of multidimensional memory:

- The way a smell can transport you
- The déjà vu that feels more like time folding
- The flash of a dream that comes true
- The knowing that doesn't come from this life

This isn't "woo." This is the quantum field in action. Your soul has always operated across dimensions. Now, science is just starting to catch up.

The Remembering Has Begun

The fact that photons can exist in 37 dimensions isn't just a curiosity. It's a message. A reflection. A **reminder** that the soul — like light — doesn't forget. Even when the mind does. Even when the world tells you to shut it down. You were never just matter. You were never just human. You are a being of light. And the light remembers.

Chapter 19

"You're not stuck in a loop. You're riding a spiral through space."

The Solar System Isn't Circling — It's Spiraling

Did you know…our solar system doesn't spin in place like a record player? That's the version most of us were taught in school — planets going 'round and 'round in flat circles. But the truth is far more dynamic…and far more magical. Because the **sun itself is moving** — racing around the Milky Way at roughly **500,000 miles per hour** — every planet orbiting the sun is also being carried forward in that motion. Which means we're not spinning in place. We're **spiraling through the galaxy**.

A Corkscrew Through the Cosmos

Visualize it: The sun is flying forward at tremendous speed Each planet is dancing around it in orbit. But because the sun is moving, the planets create beautiful, **vortex-like spirals** trailing behind it. Not flat. Not static. But living motion. You and I — right now — are **moving through space** in a giant spiral, carried by solar and galactic forces we can barely comprehend.

What This Means for Us

This isn't just astronomy. It's **remembrance**. Because that spiral movement reflects something much deeper:
We don't just repeat the same paths in life. We spiral — revisiting things **from new vantage points**

Just like the Earth orbits the sun without ever returning to the same place. It's not a perfect circle. It's an **evolving spiral** — one that rises, expands, ascends. That's how life grows. That's how healing works. That's how your soul moves.

The Spiral of the Cosmos = The Spiral of Consciousness

Everything in the universe seems to echo this:
• **Galaxies** spin in spirals
• Tornadoes, seashells, and sunflowers form spirals
DNA coils in a double helix — a spiral of biological memory
Even our **time** is spiral-shaped, returning with new frequency and flavor
So it makes sense that our solar system — and our evolution — would follow the same pattern. We aren't stuck. We aren't looping. We're spiraling forward — with each turn opening to something new.

From Flat Model to Living Mystery

The old "flat solar system" model mirrors how we used to see ourselves: Static. Predictable. Trapped in cycles. But this spiral model opens something **bigger**: we're in motion, we're part of a cosmic dance, and we're not where we were last year, last lifetime, or even yesterday.

We're evolving through the spiral of space — and of self. When I first learned this, I was stunned. How had no one taught us this? It felt like a cosmic mirror for my own life — all the times I thought I was circling back to the same place, when in fact I was moving forward, spiraling into something new.

Chapter 20

"Water is not just a substance. It is a witness."

The Water Remembers

We've been taught to think of water as a simple element — H²O, a neutral medium for life. But water is more than hydration. Water is **memory**. Across cultures, water has always been seen as sacred:

- Rivers as the blood of the Earth
- Wells as gateways to the underworld
- Oceans as the cradle of creation
- Rain as blessing and renewal

It's no accident that baptism, cleansing, and rebirth rituals center on water. We feel it instinctively: water carries more than molecules. It carries stories.

The "Aquatic Empire" Memory

When the Kamchatka quake struck, when tsunamis rippled across oceans, when I began dreaming of lost coastlines, I started hearing a phrase over and over: **"The Aquatic Empire."** I didn't invent it. It arrived.

What if our myths of **Atlantis**, **Lemuria**, or under sea civilizations are not fantasies but **collective memories** stored in the water itself — like a record etched in liquid crystal?

Modern science hints at this. Researchers like Masaru Emoto photographed how water molecules shift their structure when exposed to sound, emotion, or intention. More recently, physicists have found that water has unusual quantum properties — coherence, memory, and responsiveness to subtle fields. If light can hold 37 dimensions, maybe water can hold time.

Water as Spiral Memory

Look at the shape of a whirlpool. A hurricane. A seashell. A wave curling to shore. Water naturally spirals. It carries movement, resonance, and pattern.

Perhaps that's why, when civilizations rise and fall, the water keeps the story. Long after stone crumbles and metal rusts, the oceans still move with ancient codes. What if your own tears are part of that same remembering? What if your body — 60% water — is itself a living archive?

Why This Matters Now

As the Earth shifts, the oceans are waking too:
- Ice melts reveal ancient microbes
- Sea levels rise and reshape coasts
- New undersea volcanic activity churns the deep

More people dream of floods, whales, dolphins, and lost cities It isn't just climate change. It's memory surfacing. The water remembers.

Your Place in the Current

To work with this isn't to fear it. It's to listen. Next time you stand by a river, or touch the sea, or sip a glass of water, remember: This isn't inert matter. This is life carrying life, story carrying story. And you — like the water — are part of a vast, spiraling continuum. You are not drowning. You are remembering. And the water remembers with you.

Chapter 21

"The spiral belongs to creation. Darkness can only mimic it — never own it."

Reclaiming the Spiral

The spiral is one of the oldest sacred symbols on Earth. It is written into galaxies, into seashells, into your own DNA. It belongs to no one — and yet it lives in everything. But in recent times, this symbol — like so many sacred things — has been **co-opted** by darkness.

Some have twisted it. Used it in grotesque ways. Associated it with exploitation, with harm, with shadows that should never have touched something so pure. And for a moment, even I questioned whether I should still use it. Should I feature the spiral at all? Should I avoid the shape, the pattern, the language — out of fear of being misunderstood?

But then I remembered: That fear is the very tool they use to keep truth hidden. They want us to forget the spiral's original purpose — because remembering it is powerful.

The Spiral Is Not Theirs

They didn't create the spiral. They only **mimicked** it. They only stole it — to try to own what cannot be owned. The spiral is sacred geometry. It is how galaxies form. It is how time expands. It is how your soul remembers. The spiral is the unfolding of life itself — ever returning, ever rising, ever becoming more whole. To let fear silence this symbol would be to surrender something holy.

There's a reason the spiral has been misused. Because it's powerful. Because it's sacred. Because it works. Symbols don't just carry meaning — they carry frequency. And those who seek to manipulate often co-opt what is ancient and pure to twist it for their own ends.

This Is A Reclamation

So I speak this clearly, now: This book does not use the spiral as a symbol of harm. It uses it as it was always meant to be used — as a symbol of **creation**, **growth**, **awakening**, and **truth**. This is not a symbol of darkness. This is a symbol of light — and of the **journey toward it**. So I reclaim it. I reclaim it for the soul that is healing. For the child within you who is awakening. For the ancient part of you that always knew what it meant. Let this spiral be what it always was: A remembrance. A return. A rising.

Living the Spiral

The spiral is not only an idea or a symbol. It is a way of living. It is how you move through your days, your relationships, your challenges, and your becoming. To live the spiral is to stop expecting life to be linear — and to begin trusting the echoes that return.

You do not have to master this all at once. You do not have to walk it perfectly. You only have to notice when the spiral calls you back — and remember that each return is a chance to rise, soften, or see more clearly than before.

The spiral will bring you to thresholds, but it will also meet you in the ordinary: in a conversation that stirs an old wound, in a sunrise that feels like déjà vu, in a choice that asks whether you will abandon yourself or stand in truth. These are not detours. They are spiral moments — invitations to live awake.

In my recent journey, I've been listening to a teacher who often repeats a simple phrase: "I Am That I Am." At first, it sounds almost too simple, but the more I sat with it, the more I realized it's the heart of this spiral. The past may echo through memories, the future is not yet written — but right here, in this present moment, the truth of who we are never changes. "I Am That I Am" is not about ego. It's about remembering that the divine lives in us now, not someday, not if we earn it, but here. Each time the spiral circles back, it asks us: Will you forget again, or will you stand in "*I Am?*"

Below are simple reflections, affirmations, and practices to anchor the spiral in your everyday life. Let them be companions. You don't need to use them all. Choose what stirs you. Trust that the spiral will guide you to what you need.

Reflections

- Where in my life do I feel like I'm "back where I started"?
- How is this return different from the last time I was here?
- What lesson or gift might this spiral be offering me now?

Affirmations

- *I trust the spiral of my becoming.*
- *I am not repeating. I am returning wiser, stronger, and more whole.*
- *Each echo carries me closer to my truth.*

Journaling Prompts

- Describe a recent spiral moment — a trigger, a joy, a déjà vu. How did you meet it?
- What would it look like to walk that same spiral with more compassion for yourself?
- Write a letter to your past self, from the higher place you stand on the spiral now.

Everyday Practices

Pause in Spiral Moments — when something feels familiar, stop and ask: *What's different this time?*

Trace Spirals — doodle spirals in the margins, on scrap paper, or in your journal. Let your hand remember what your mind forgets.

Walk a Spiral Path — if you find a labyrinth, walk it slowly. If not, create one with stones or simply with your finger on paper.

• **Speak to the Echo** — when an old wound resurfaces, whisper to yourself: *This is an echo. It is not who I am now.*

"You are not broken. You are remembering. That remembering is the law of life."

Closing Blessing

Last night, as I sat outside in the cold searching for the Andromeda galaxy, I felt both awe and sorrow. Awe at the beauty spread across the sky, and sorrow that I hadn't been shown this way of seeing when I was young. If I had grown up with the stars as my teachers instead of the limits of doctrine and dogma, I might have awakened sooner. But the spiral has carried me here, in its own time. It circled me back to what was almost stolen so that I could reclaim it now. That is the gift of the spiral: no matter how many times we forget, it brings us home again — to wonder, to love, to remembrance.

So, I ask that you remember that you are not behind. You are not broken or repeating. You are returning. The spiral will keep calling you, not to punish you, but to remind you that remembering is real. Every echo you hear is proof of your becoming.

This is not the end of your awakening. It is a resting point in the spiral — a place to breathe, to pause, and to feel what has settled…and what is still rising. You have walked through memory. You have sat with symbols. You have tuned your frequency. You have re-met yourself — soul first. And now, you carry this with you — not as doctrine, but as a *companion*.

There will be days when you forget. There will be moments when you question. There will be spirals that pull you deeper than you expected. Let that be okay. You do not have to hold it all at once. You only have to **remember that remembering is real**.

Let this book be a breadcrumb. A whisper. A witness. The spiral will bring you back when it's time. And you...will know the way.

Epilogue

"Synchronicities are not coincidences. They are the spiral speaking in the language of timing."

For most of my life, I thought synchronicities were just "special signs" — like feathers, numbers, or a song playing on the radio when I needed encouragement. And while those moments still touch me deeply, I've learned they are only the beginning. Synchronicities are not random gifts. They are living echoes — feedback loops that show us when we're in alignment, when we're being nudged, and when we're being carried.

It's easy to miss them because they rarely shout. They arrive quietly — in the timing of a word, in the smile of a stranger, in a child's laughter at the very moment you're about to cry. They show up when you are stressed and suddenly notice a flower blooming, or a song that softens your heart. The spiral moves through everything, even the smallest details, reminding us that life is listening.

Just the other day, I was questioning if all this work — the writing, the preparing, and the endless tasks — was really worth it. Before I could even finish the thought, my husband interrupted me. "No. Keep going," he said. "What can I do to help?"

I told him about the Christmas photo project I had barely begun. I had the backdrop, but nothing else. Before I could blink, he was climbing into the attic, hauling down the tree, the ornaments, the boxes of decorations. He brought in my antique wagon and started setting up a scene. Then he went out searching for antique toys to pose in the wagon.

That is synchronicity, too. Not just numbers or signs, but love taking form in the moment you most need it.

Synchronicities are the spiral in real time. They confirm, they encourage, they remind. They may arrive through a tarot reading at 11:11, or a dragonfly crossing your path, or a partner quietly carrying part of your burden without you asking. They are all echoes of the same truth: you are not forgotten, you are not alone, and you are exactly where you need to be.

Where in your life have synchronicities appeared lately? What might they be echoing back to you about your path?

Appendix

"The spiral doesn't just teach — it invites. And it never forces."

Practices from the Spiral

The soul's path is nonlinear. It returns. It repeats. It deepens. And if you begin to notice, you'll see the spiral everywhere — in your healing, your relationships, your choices, your creations.

These practices are not requirements. They are reminders — soft invitations to help you align with the spiral when you feel lost, disconnected, or overwhelmed. You don't need to master them. You only need to meet them where you are.

1. Walk a Spiral (or Labyrinth)
Find or draw a simple spiral or labyrinth pattern. Walk it slowly — either physically (if you have space) or with your finger on the page.
As you walk in: Let go of expectations. Notice what arises. Listen for what your soul is ready to release. At the center, pause. Breathe. Ask: "What am I ready to remember?" As you spiral outward, feel yourself integrating — not just healing, but embodying.

2. Create a Soul Spiral Map
On a blank sheet, draw a wide spiral with 5–7 turns. Label each turn with a key return point in your life — moments where you "looped back" to something you thought was finished:

- A pattern

- A person
- A lesson
- A trigger
- A calling

Ask: What did I learn the second (or third) time through? What changed in me? This helps you reframe "repetition" as evolution in motion.

3. Use Spiral Doodling as Meditation
The next time you're restless or can't hear your inner voice, try this: Set a timer for 5–10 minutes. With pen or pencil, begin drawing slow, continuous spirals. Let your hand move freely. Don't judge. Don't edit. Just spiral.

Notice what arises. What feelings move? What thoughts settle? Sometimes the spiral opens a space that words can't.

4. Recognize a Spiral Moment in Real Time
Whenever you feel like you're "back where you started," pause and ask:
- What's familiar about this situation?
- But what's different about how I'm meeting it now?
- Is this truly a repeat — or is it a return with new eyes?

This turns frustration into a sacred checkpoint.

5. Affirmation for the Path
- I trust the spiral of my becoming.
- I am not behind. I am not lost.

- I am returning — deeper, wiser, and more whole each time.

Say it aloud. Write it on your mirror. Whisper it when doubt creeps in because you're not failing. You're just spiraling home.

Spiral Timeline Worksheet

Tracking the Echoes of Your Life

The spiral of life often circles us back to familiar places — old wounds, recurring fears, repeating lessons. This worksheet is designed to help you notice those echoes, not as failures, but as invitations to see what's different this time.

Step 1: Identify the Echo
What keeps returning in your life?
- Jealousy, worry, fear, or self-image?
- A relationship dynamic that repeats?
- A health issue or physical symptom?
- A dream, synchronicity, or symbol?

Step 2: Mark the Spirals
A free downloadable Reflection Worksheet for this section is available at RootedHoundPress.com/echoesworksheet

Step 3: Notice the Spiral
- Look across your entries. Ask yourself:
- How is my response shifting over time?
- What wisdom have I gained that wasn't there before?

- What is the spiral teaching me as it circles back?

Write a short note to yourself from your current place on the spiral:

"Dear Self, I see how this echo has followed me. I honor how I used to respond, and I celebrate how I respond now. Each return is not a punishment — it is proof of my becoming."